MY VERY OWN BOOK OF

MOTORCYCLES

Designed by

Motorcycle design

Germany was the birthplace of the motorcycle. Gottlieb Daimler developed the first gasoline-powered motorcycle in 1885. In 1894, Hildebrand and Wolfmüller started to produce four-cylinder motorcycles. Today, BMW is the only survivor of a once massive German motorcycle industry. Italian motorcycles have gained a reputation for their inspired design and impressive racing achievements. Garelli and Ducati made many road and commuter bikes in huge quantities.

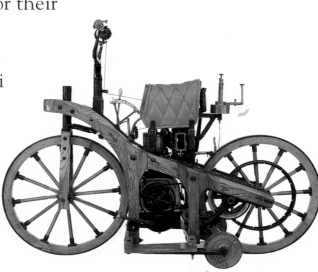

Pedal power
A scooter is an easy-to-ride small-wheeled bike that is cheap to run. Most scooters cannot go as fast as motorcycles, but they are still fun to ride.

The first motorcycle
Did you know that motorcycles have existed for as long as cars – over 100 years? Gottlieb Daimler, one of the inventors of the car, made the first true motorcycle in 1885. He did this by fixing an engine to a bicycle frame.

Bimota
Bimota makes 300 hand-finished motorcycles each year. The bikes are exclusively designed, which makes them very expensive.

Cross-country racing
The MZ 1SDT was widely used for cross-country sporting events. Specialized machines were used by East Germans and other teams to win many medals in this grueling sport.

Gilera Saturno
This Gilera Saturno model was built in the late 1980s. It was originally aimed at the Japanese market, but was eventually sold worldwide.

Bacon slicer
The famous "bacon slicer" flywheel was a notable feature of Moto Guzzi's big single-cylinder machines until the late 1960s. The engine was also used to power a popular three-wheeled truck.

Ducati
The 851 is the most complex Ducati ever built. It utilized four camshafts, eight valves, a water cooling system, and fuel injection.

A bit more room
Riding a motorcycle with a sidecar is not like riding a solo machine. The handlebars must be physically pulled to change direction and the sidecar will try to overtake the bike when braking.

Werner motorcycle
Russian brothers Eugene and Michel Werner experimented with motorcycles in Paris. Their 1901 Werner model had a carburetor, wheelrim brakes, and electric ignition. All these features made it one of the first truly practical motorcycles.

Motorcycles from Europe

European countries such as France, Belgium, and Czechoslovakia once boasted a significant motorcycle industry. But many companies closed in the 1950s and 1960s, after a long period of decline. The prosperity of a nation's economy contributes to the decline of the industry because it means that more people can afford to buy cars in greater numbers than motorcycles.

Montesa
Montesa was founded in 1944 by Pedro Permanyer and Francisco Bulto in Spain. A Montesa won the World Trials Championship in 1980.

Trial tester
Trial bikes such as the Bultaco Sherpa from Spain make almost any terrain passable. Trials are one of the oldest forms of motorcycle sport. A trial event tests the rider's skill in mastering a series of obstacles.

Deronzière
In France, Deronzière produced motorcycles from 1903 until the outbreak of World War I. They used their own 282cc engines, and also used motors supplied by Peugeot.

Husqvarna Motocross
The Swedish Husqvarna is designed especially for motocross racing. This event involves racing around a field through mud and over bumps. Motocross racing is very popular in the United States, where the national championship is known as "Super Cross."

Böhmerland
The unusual Böhmerland motorcycle from Czechoslovakia could seat up to three people. Its production was halted with the outbreak of World War II.

EARLY MOTORCYCLES

1921 Velocette D2 (Italy)

1919 Model E BSA (UK)

1885 Moto Guzzi 500S (Italy)

1885 Daimler (Germany)

1936 Harley-Davidson
Knucklehead 61E (US)

1901 Werner (Germany)

1928 Moto Guzzi 500S (Italy)

FN (Belgium)

1923 Douglas
and Dixon
Banking Sidecar
(UK)

Working Motorcycles

1991 Honda GL1500/6
Gold Wing (Japan)

1966 Triumph Saint (UK)

1963 Vespa
Grand Sport
160 Mark 1
(Italy)

1957
Lambretta
LD150 (Italy)

1942
Harley-
Davidson
WLA
(US)

1971 BMW R75/5 (Germany)

1915 Autoped (US)

1965 BMW R/60
with 1952 Steib
chair (Germany)

Harley-Davidson
WLA, 1942 (US)

The
Honda logo
is a single wing

1979
Kawasaki
KR750
(Japan)

A mudguard for
a Gilera Saturno

1992 Rotary Norton
NRS588 (UK)

1984 Honda
RS500 (Japan)

1983 Heysercycle (Japan)

1992 Suzuki RGV500 (Japan)

1976 Benelli 750 Sei (Italy)

1979 Kawasaki Z1300 (Japan)

1980 Honda CBX1000 (Japan)

1989 Gilera
Saturno
(Italy)

1982 Suzuki
Katana
(Japan)

MODERN MOTORCYCLES

The early
Kawasaki logo

1992 Yamaha FZR
1000 Exup (Japan)

1992 BMW K1
(Germany)

The Laverda logo

1982 Laverda
Jota 180 (Italy)

Suzuki RGV500
(Japan)

1989 Ducati 851 (Italy)

The BSA logo

1983 Kawasaki ZX750 (Japan)

1992 Montesa Cota (Spain)

1992
Bimota
Tesi 1D
(Italy)

1985 MZ
1SDT
(Germany)

RACING MOTORCYCLES

1968 Kirby BSA Racing Sidecar (UK)

1971
Triumph
Trident (UK)

1981 Weslake Speedway (UK)

1938
Manx
Norton
(UK)

1977 Kawasaki
2400cc Dragster
(Japan)

1964 Bultaco
Sherpa (Spain)

1978 Yamaha
OW48
(Japan)

1948 Indian 648
Scout (US)

1992
Husqvarna
Motocross
TC610
(Sweden)

EARLY MOTORCYCLES

1901 NSU (Germany)

1910 Yale (US)

Claude Temple
wore this helmet
when racing in
the 1920s

This helmet
was worn by
Graham Walker

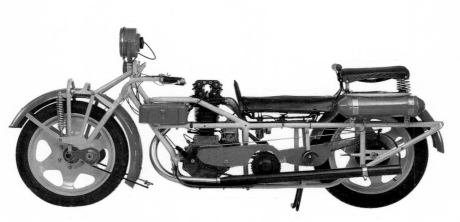

1927 Böhmerland (Czechoslovakia)

Mike Hailwood
wore this helmet
when racing on
an MV Augusta

1904 Indian Single (US)

1907 Deronzière (France)

1912 Norton BS "Old Miracle" (UK)

1923 Temple-Anzani (UK)

American motorcycles

The first American motorcycles appeared at the turn of the century. Pioneer American motorcyclists needed rugged, reliable machines able to cover great distances on rough roads. In 1914, the V-twin was established as the most popular American motorcycle engine. Harley-Davidson, Indian, Excelsior, and others all adopted this engine layout.

Standing room only
The versatile American-made Autoped was produced in 1915. It had no seat and had to be driven standing up! When folded, it could fit in the trunk of a car.

Rugged runner
The 1904 Indian Single was the first motorcycle built by George Hendee and Oscar Hedstrom. Its sound engineering was combined with the vital ruggedness needed for tough road conditions.

Military motorcycle
The simple and rugged "Forty-Five" was an ideal military motorcycle. Based on the civilian machine, the army version was cheaper, stronger, and just as reliable.

Classic Yale
Yale motorcycles were produced in Ohio from 1902 until 1915. The company became well known for its big 950cc V-twin engine, equipped with a two-speed gearbox and chain drive to the rear wheel.

Wall-of-death
The Indian 101 Scout was a favorite with stunt riders, especially those who performed the "wall-of-death." This stunt involved riding around the top of a circular wooden drum. The stunt rider avoided falling off by gathering enough speed to defy gravity.

Japanese motorcycles

Today, Japan is the world's biggest producer of motorcycles in the world. The industry prides itself in providing different motorcycles for every corner of the market. The most famous Japanese motorcycle producers, known as the "big four," are Honda, Suzuki, Yamaha, and Kawasaki. Japanese motorcycles have a reputation for being clean, reliable, and fun to ride.

Winged leader
Honda was founded by Soichiro Honda in 1948. Honda's first motorized bicycle was such a success that by the mid-1950s, it led the home market. By the mid-1960s, it dominated the world market.

Drag racer
This Kawasaki dragster reaches a top speed of 186 mph (300 km/h). Because enormous power output is required, the engine does not last for long. Usually it has to be rebuilt after each race.

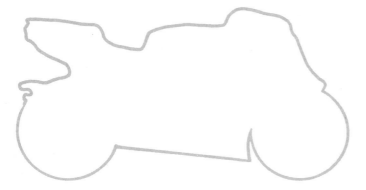

Hang in there
A Grand Prix racing motorcycle can reach a top speed of 185 mph (298 km/h). When the racers turn corners, they lean over so far that their knees sometimes touch the ground. The faster they go around the corners, the more they have to lean.

Suzuki Katana
The Katana reaches a top speed of 140 mph (225 km/h). Katana is the name of the Japanese samurai sword that appears on the logo.

Kawasaki
Kawasaki builds high performance
motorcycles for enthusiasts. But
it is the smallest of the big
four Japanese manufacturers.

Superbike
Superbikes are designed to have the best
possible handling under racing conditions.
Wayne Rainey won the 1983 American
Superbike Championship on this Kawasaki.

Industrial giant
Apart from making
motorcycles, Kawasaki
produces aircraft, robots, bridges, and
boats. In fact, motorcycles only make up
a small part of the company's total output.

Winged luxury
Some people think the Gold Wing
is the ultimate two-wheeled luxury
motorcycle. This example is the
500,000th Honda to be built in America.

Go for green
Green is the traditional
Kawasaki racing color. This
KR750 reaches a top
speed of 150 mph
(241 km/h).

What a winner!
Yamaha motorcycles have set high
standards of performance and
reliability. From 1961 to 1968, Yamahas
won several world championships.

Honda racer
Honda made a spectacular
comeback in the 1979
Grand Prix. In 1983,
Honda went on to win
the World Championship.

British motorcycles

Pioneering British companies such as Norton, BSA, and Triumph had a reputation for innovation and manufacturing excellence. Most of the British motorcycle industry was based around Coventry and Birmingham. This location soon became known as the "workshop of the world."

Old-fashioned miracle
The Norton BS could speed around a racetrack at 70 mph (113 km/h). Between 1912 and 1920, it set 112 national speed records.

Manx Norton racer
The Manx Norton raced in the annual Tourist Trophy race. This race takes place on public roads in the Isle of Man off the northwest coast of Britain. The races began in 1907 and still continue today.

Speed king
Claude Temple was the first person to cover 100 miles (160 km) in one hour on a motorcycle.

BSA
The Birmingham Small Arms Company built its first motorcycles in 1906, and became Britain's biggest manufacturer. The BSA Model E was cheap, reliable, and popular, especially when used with a sidecar.

Racing sidecar
The driver and passenger of a sidecar work together as a team; the passenger adjusts his weight to control wheel spin and help gain traction. On some tracks, machines with sidecars can be faster than solo machines.

Record breaker
This Temple-Anzani was built in 1923. In October of that year it set a speed record of 108 mph (174 km/h) on the Brooklands racetrack.